Imitating *Nature*

From **Boxfish** to
Aerodynamic **Cars**

Toney Allman

KIDHAVEN PRESS

An imprint of Thomson Gale, a part of The Thomson Corporation

THOMSON

™

GALE

Detroit • New York • San Francisco • San Diego • New Haven, Conn. • Waterville, Maine • London • Munich

FX.11-12

LIBRARY OF CONGRESS CATALOGING-IN-PUBLICATION DATA

Allman, Toney.
　From boxfish to aerodynamic cars / by Toney Allman.
　　p. cm. — (Imitating nature)
　Includes bibliographical references and index.
　ISBN 0-7377-3609-7 (hard cover : alk. paper) 1. Automobiles—Aerodynamics—Juvenile literature. 2. Boxfishes—Juvenile literature. 3. Inventions—Juvenile literature. 4. Imitation—Juvenile literature. I. Title. II. Series.
　TL245.A57 2006
　629.2'31— dc22
　　　　　　　　　　　　　　　　　　　　　　　　　　　2006000747

Printed in China

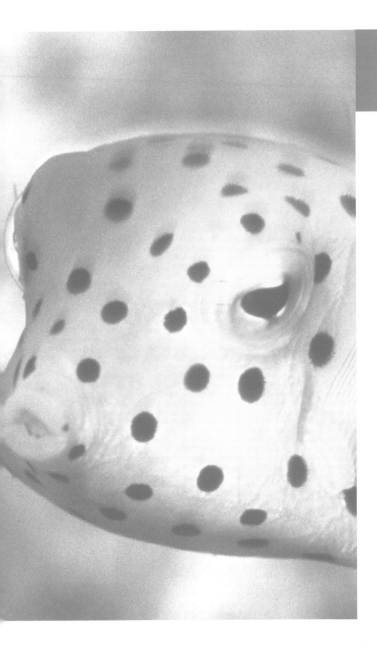

Contents

CHAPTER 1

Boxy Is Best

Researchers at DaimlerChrysler in Germany wanted to invent a new kind of Mercedes-Benz car that imitated nature. They thought a car that imitated an animal would be efficient and speedy. It would be **streamlined**, with a sleek, smooth, even shape. It would also save energy and be environmentally friendly. They searched for a model in nature to copy.

The researchers examined sharks, penguins, and dolphins that speed through water with streamlined shapes. Maybe, they thought, a car could speed through air in the same way animals swim through water. Cars, however, have to have room inside for seats, head space, and legroom. The torpedo shapes of streamlined animals would not do for normal-sized, rectangular cars. Then, the researchers discovered the yellow boxfish. It does not look streamlined. It is shaped like a box, but it turned out to be the perfect model for creating a new kind of car.

The yellow boxfish is a surprisingly good model for an energy-friendly car.

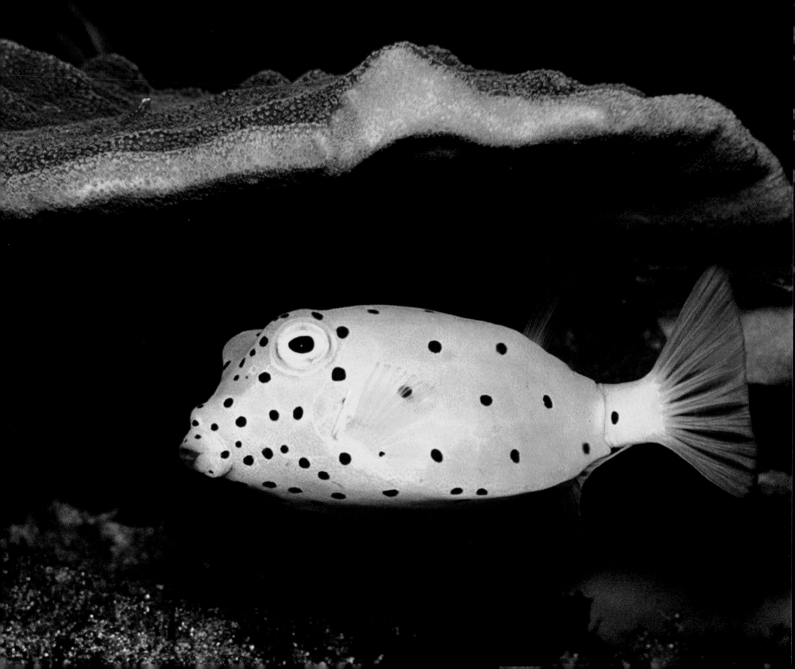

Handle with Care

Boxfish are also called cowfish or trunkfish. They are members of the puffer fish family. Like all puffers, they are able to release a poison into the water when they are frightened or need to protect themselves. Boxfish are usually gentle, though, and rarely try to poison the researchers who study them.

A frightened boxfish will puff out its body and release poison into the water.

In the Coral Reefs

Yellow boxfish are bright yellow with dark spots and grow to be about 17.5 inches (45cm) long. They live in tropical waters near places such as Australia, Fiji, and the Philippines. Their bodies are coated with hard, bony, six-sided plates that form a protective armor called a **carapace**. This carapace makes boxfish bodies rigid and stiff. Boxfish cannot wiggle easily, but even so, they are expert swimmers. They can swim six body lengths in one second; make quick, darting turns; and stay balanced and stable in the tumbling, rolling waters where they make their homes.

Boxfish live in shallow water around rocky coral reefs, where ocean waves and currents are rough. The boxfish's hard carapace protects it from injuries, but it is not knocked into things very often. It swims skillfully around the reefs, catching food or escaping from enemies.

Boxes and Beads

A team of university scientists wanted to understand how boxfish shapes help them to swim so easily in rough water. Some of the scientists were Daniel Weihs from Israel's Technion University, Ian Bartol of the University of California in Los Angeles, Paul Webb from the University of Michigan, and Morteza Gharib at California Institute of Technology. In several experiments, the scientists built plastic models of boxfish and placed them in water tanks that were full of tiny, colored beads. They turned on artificial waves and used cameras to film the beads and water as they flowed over the models. The beads made it possible to see exactly how the water acted as it hit the box shapes.

Like other boxfish, the white-barred boxfish of Australia has protective armor called a carapace. The hard, bony armor can be seen in this close-up view.

How Boxfish Stay Balanced

Boxfish can remain balanced while swimming in rough water currents because little whirlpools, called leading-edge vortices (or LEVs), form on the front corners of their boxy shapes. The LEVs form at the bottom and top of the fish and grow larger as they move along its body.

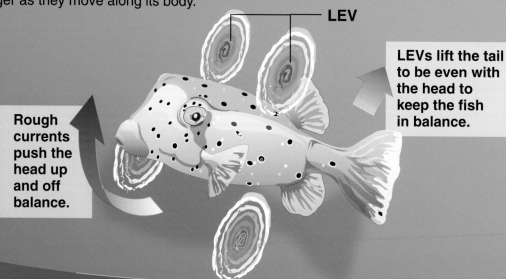

LEV

LEVs lift the tail to be even with the head to keep the fish in balance.

Rough currents push the head up and off balance.

When the boxfish swims up, LEVs develop at its four "edges," or keels. The vortices move along the fish's body and pull the tail end of the fish up. This helps keep the fish level and stable.

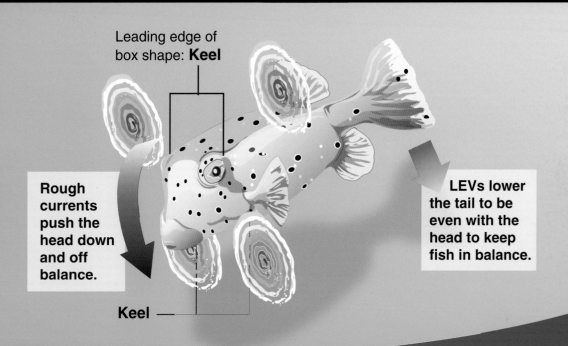

Leading edge of
box shape: **Keel**

**Rough
currents
push the
head down
and off
balance.**

**LEVs lower
the tail to be
even with the
head to keep
fish in balance.**

Keel —

In a downward dive, the boxfish generates vortices that help pull
the tail end of the fish down (orange arrow).

Vortex Means Whirlpool

After years of work, the scientific team discovered the boxfish's secret for staying stable. At the top and bottom edges of the box shape, little swirly whirlpools of water are formed as the fish swims through flowing water. These whirlpools, called **leading-edge vortices**, grow larger as they move along the body of the fish. They hold the fish balanced in the water, no matter how rough it gets.

If the fish's head is pitched upward by a wave, the strong whirlpools near its tail suck up the tail to be even with the head. If the head is pitched downward, the vortices suck the tail down. Boxfish have to move their fins very little to stay balanced or to avoid pitching from side to side or back and forth while they swim. The leading-edge vortices around their boxy shapes keep them safely swimming no matter where they dart or what the water conditions are. The whirlpools formed by the flow of water make the boxfish's hard, boxy body very streamlined.

Fins and Whirlpools

Boxfish have five fins that they use to propel themselves through the water. Since the leading-edge vortices keep them steady, they do not need to use their fins very often to fight ocean waves or stay still in one place. With their strong fin muscles, however, boxfish can swim fast and powerfully when necessary.

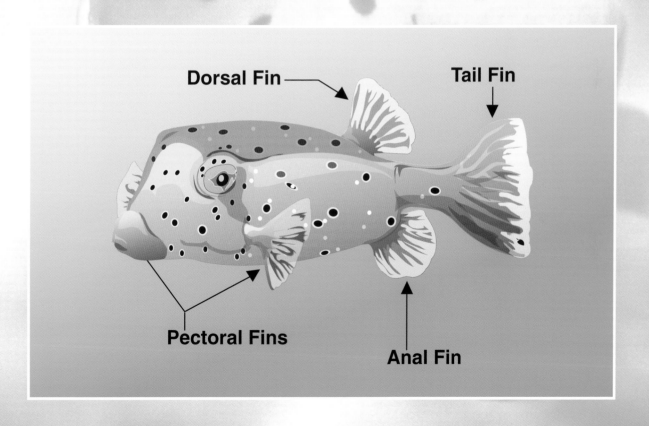

Dorsal Fin

Tail Fin

Pectoral Fins

Anal Fin

No Flopping Around

Daniel Weihs says that leading-edge vortices help a boxfish to be a faster swimmer. He explains in an interview with the author, "**By preventing unnecessary rocking motions, the drag is reduced . . . so that indirectly it helps the fish move faster.**"

Just Right for a Car?

When DaimlerChrysler researchers learned about the benefits of boxy shapes, they were excited. Boxfish are almost the same rectangular shape as the inside of car bodies. The researchers decided to see if imitating boxfish would make a streamlined, energy-saving, stable car.

CHAPTER 2

Fish, Raindrops, and Clay

Engineers are researchers and scientists who design and build inventions and new structures. Before Mercedes-Benz engineers could build a boxfish car, however, they had to do experiments to see if their idea would work.

Built to Travel

One project engineer, Dieter Gurtler, believed that boxfish are a lot like cars. He said all boxfish are missing is wheels. Boxfish, for instance, need to be streamlined so they can move easily through water. Cars have to be streamlined to move through the air. As they swim through water, boxfish have to be able to make sharp turns in the rocky reefs where they live. Cars must turn easily, too, and be stable enough not to turn over.

Bumping into things could be dangerous for both boxfish and cars. If boxfish accidentally knock into

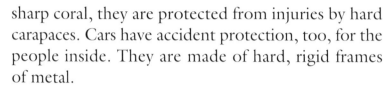

Boxfish glide easily through the water because of their streamlined shape.

sharp coral, they are protected from injuries by hard carapaces. Cars have accident protection, too, for the people inside. They are made of hard, rigid frames of metal.

Another way that cars and boxfish are alike is that both need fuel. Cars use gas, and a boxfish's fuel is its food. Cars and boxfish need to use their fuel efficiently and not waste it. If boxfish waste fuel and energy, they will not survive. When cars waste energy, it is expensive and bad for the environment.

The most important way that boxfish and cars are alike is their shape. Boxfish are rectangular, with only sharp, bulging noses and big eyes sticking out in front of them. Cars are basically rectangles, also. People sit inside the rectangle, with hood and headlights sticking out in front.

From Boxfish to Aerodynamic Cars

But Are They Aerodynamic?

Boxfish appeared to be great models for building cars, but Gurtler and the other engineers needed to be sure. They had to figure out the **aerodynamic efficiency** of boxfish shapes. Aerodynamic efficiency is a measure of how easily and stably a shape can slip through the air. If it cuts through the air with ease, it is aerodynamically efficient. Aerodynamics is a measure of slipperiness.

If the air slows down an object, that is called **drag**. A person who sticks an open hand out a moving car's window is feeling the drag of the air. Like a hand, a car shape that is not streamlined has a lot of drag and is slowed down by the air it is pushing through. Drag wastes fuel and energy.

A Global Effort

The main headquarters for the Mercedes-Benz Technology Center and the DaimlerChrysler research laboratory are in Stuttgart, Germany. The German engineers worked with many other scientists around the world to develop the bionic car.

Engineers in Germany work on developing a new Mercedes-Benz car.

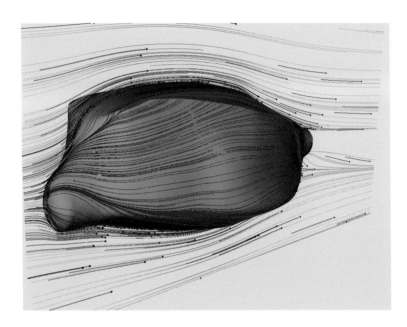

This illustration shows the aerodynamic efficiency of a boxfish clay model in the wind tunnel tests. Air flows smoothly around the shape.

Compared to a Raindrop

The most perfect aerodynamic shape, with almost no drag, is a shape in nature —the raindrop. A water droplet is so slippery that air hardly slows it down as it falls. The engineers did an experiment to compare the aerodynamic efficiency of boxfish to the raindrop shape. They built a clay model of a boxfish. They put the clay model in a water tank, where they made water rush over it. They put it in a wind tunnel, where they blew wind at it. Then they measured how easily the water and air flowed over the clay boxfish. They discovered that the boxfish shape, with its leading-edge vortices, was almost as aerodynamically efficient as a raindrop. It was very slippery and had little drag.

The engineers were pleased. They decided to build a clay model of a car that was shaped as much as possible like a boxfish. The model was one-fourth the

From Boxfish to Aerodynamic Cars

size of a real car. The engineers placed the model in their wind and water tunnels and measured its aerodynamics. The car model was not as efficient as the actual boxfish shape, but it was close. It was much more aerodynamically efficient than any cars on the road today.

Let's Do It!

The DaimlerChrysler engineers had proof that boxfish were the perfect animals to imitate. They were ready to build a real car with as many of the same qualities of the clay model as possible.

The engineers built a clay model of a boxfish (top) to test the aerodynamics of the shape and then built a clay car (bottom) for more testing.

CHAPTER 3

The Bionic Car

In 2005 the engineering team at DaimlerChrysler finished the Mercedes-Benz bionic car. *Bionic* means combining biology and technology. The bionic car is the first in the world that imitates an animal. It is a strange-looking car, but it is aerodynamically efficient, safe, and stable.

Boxfish Car

Its appearance may be unusual, but the bionic car is a practical compact car with two doors and seats for four people. It is 13.9 feet (4.24m) long, 6 feet (1.8m) wide, and 5.2 feet (1.6m) high. It is shaped like a rectangle. It has a small, bulging nose and an angular, sharp-edged body that sweeps back to a wide, squared-off tail. Its windshield extends up over the roof, becoming a sunroof. Its shape is as close as possible to that of a boxfish.

How Aerodynamic Is It?

Aerodynamics and drag are measured by a number called a "drag coefficient" or Cd value. The lower the number, the smaller the drag, and the slipperier the object. Any human made object with a Cd value of 0.09 or lower is considered highly aerodynamic.

A raindrop's Cd value is 0.04.   **The clay boxfish model has a Cd value of 0.06.**   **The clay car model's Cd value is 0.095.**

The Mercedez-Benz Bionic Car's Cd value is higher than the model's, but still better than other cars.

Mercedez-Benz Bionic Car: Cd 0.19

Honda Insight: Cd value: 0.25   **Toyota Prius: Cd value: 0.26**   **Parachute: Cd value: 1.75**

Source: *Popular Science*

Bionic Aerodynamics

The car is not as aerodynamic as a boxfish because the engineers could not exactly imitate the clay car model in full size. However, the bionic car is more slippery and aerodynamically efficient than other compact cars. To increase the aerodynamics, the engineers added wind-reducing masks over all four of the car's wheels. Instead of side mirrors, they gave the car rearview cameras with monitors inside. This way, nothing sticks out of the car that might increase drag. Even the door handles are sunk into the doors so they will not cause any drag as the wind flows over them.

Because of its design, the bionic car is very fuel efficient and wastes little energy. The greater the drag, the harder a car must work and the more fuel it uses to push against the wind. The more aerodynamically efficient a car is, the less fuel it takes to move it along through the air. The bionic car uses 20 percent less fuel than other cars and can go about 70 miles on a gallon of gas (23.26km/l).

Tough and Speedy

The bionic car is safe and efficient, but it is also powerful, just like a boxfish. It has a top speed of 118 miles (190km/h) per hour.

The finished car (opposite) has rearview cameras inside instead of mirrors that would stick out and cause drag.

A Bionic Skeleton

The Mercedes-Benz engineers did not copy just the boxfish shape. They also imitated the carapace when they built the car's frame. The boxfish's bony plates are strong on its sides, for example, to protect it from injury, but the plates are light or even missing where no vital organs have to be protected. In this way, the boxfish weighs as little as possible and does not waste energy carrying extra weight that is not needed for safety.

The Mercedes-Benz engineers used special microscopes and computer analysis to copy a boxfish carapace when they built the bionic car's skeleton, or frame. The frame is a kind of honeycomb that is stronger than a usual car frame shape. The door skeleton, for instance, is strong and thick in some areas but thin in others where strength is not needed. This reduces the car's weight. The bionic car weighs only about 2,400 pounds (1,100kg), lighter than other cars of the same size. Because it imitates a honeycombed carapace, however, its light weight does not make it less tough. It is just as safe in crashes as any other Mercedes-Benz car.

The design of the car frame looks like the boxfish skeleton.

Driving into the Future

In June 2005, DaimlerChrysler showed off its bionic car in Washington, D.C., as an engineer drove it around RFK Stadium. Then, in November, the project's head engineer, Ralph Hettich, drove a lap in the car on the Mercedes-Benz World Brooklands Racetrack in England. People from around the world got a chance to see and admire the bionic car.

Only one bionic car has been built. It is called a concept car because it will never be for sale. The ideas used in the car, however, will be used to build improved Mercedes-Benz bionic cars in the future. Someday, perhaps, people will be able to buy a car as aerodynamically efficient as a boxfish. Dieter Gurtler said that, in the next version, engineers may even add cup holders!

The first aerodynamic car based on a boxfish is introduced to the world in 2005.

Glossary

aerodynamic efficiency: A measure of the slipperiness of, and amount of drag on, an object as it moves through gases, especially the air.

carapace: The hard, bony coating, or armor, that covers most of a boxfish body.

drag: A measure of air or water resistance as a solid body moves through it. The higher the drag, the less aerodynamic or streamlined an object is.

engineers: People who use science and math to solve practical problems and build new inventions and structures.

leading-edge vortices (LEVs): The small, spiraling whirlpools that form at the front edges of the boxfish body and keep the fish stable and aerodynamically efficient. (*Vortex* is singular, for one whirlpool, and *vortices* is plural.)

streamlined: Having a sleek, smooth shape and reduced drag.

For Further Exploration

Books

Carey Combe, ed., *Big Book of Cars*. New York: Dorling Kindersley, 1999. This beautiful book, with lots of pictures, describes some of the most unusual cars ever built. Readers can learn about James Bond's cars, the Batmobile, amazing concept cars, and fantastic cars from several different car companies that have surprising capabilities.

Salvatore Tocci, *Coral Reefs: Life Below the Sea*. Danbury, CT: Franklin Watts, 2004. Explore the abundant life in the coral reef and learn how the ecosystem survives and thrives. Boxfish are just one of many animals that are described in this book.

Web Sites

Fishes: Locomotion, Yahooligans! Animals (http://yahooligans. yahoo.com/content/animals/fishes/fishes_locomotion.html). Learn about the different ways that fish swim. Boxfish are called trunkfish in this article. Their different swimming methods and their movements are compared to other fish featured on this site.

Mercedes Bionic Concept Car, Car Buyer's Notebook (www.carbuyersnotebook.com/archives/2005/06/ mercedes_bionic.htm). This article describes the first demonstration of the bionic car in Washington, D.C. See pictures of the car, its interior, and its video monitors. Watch a short video about its design. There is even a link to download a screensaver of the bionic car.

Where the Story Begins, Mercedes-Benz Laboratory (www.mercedes-benz.com/content/mbcom/international/ international_website/en/com/international_home/home/ innovation/laboratory/researchvehicles.html). Mercedes-Benz's main research laboratory is in Germany. The bionic car is just one of a long line of innovations from the company's technology research center. Take a look at some of the pictures and descriptions of the many concept cars developed there over the years.

Index

Picture Credits

About the Author

Toney Allman has degrees from Ohio State University and the University of Hawaii. She currently lives in Virginia, where she enjoys writing books for students and learning about the natural world.